My Venus Book

By Nicholas J. D. Sims

Copyright © 2023 by Nicholas J.D. Sims

All rights reserved. This book or any portion thereof may not be reproduced or used in any manner whatsoever without the express written permission of the publisher except for the use of brief quotations in a book review.

Despite the harsh environment, Nicholas and his friends were amazed by the planet's unique features.

They learned that Venus rotates in the opposite direction to most planets, and its day is longer than its year!

After a day of exploration, Nicholas and his friends returned to Earth, filled with knowledge and awe about the planet Venus.

They shared their experiences with their friends and family, inspiring others to learn more about our neighboring planet.

Nicholas and his friends put on special suits to protect them from the extreme heat and explored the planet.

They saw mountains and valleys, just like on Earth, but they were different colors.

Venus is covered in rocks and minerals that give it a yellow and orange hue.

As they traveled deeper into the planet, Nicholas and his friends saw that it was covered in thick clouds.

But instead of being white and fluffy, like Earth's clouds, these clouds were made of sulfuric acid, making them dangerous to breathe.

And from that day on, Nicholas and his friends dreamed of future missions to Venus, where they could continue to learn about this remarkable planet and unravel its mysteries.

ABOUT THE AUTHOR

My name is Nicholas Joseph David Sims. I am five years old. I have two dogs one named Mercury and the other named Bolt. Sometimes I call Bolt Venus as his nick name. My nick name is Nicholatte. My birthday is December 2nd, 2017. I started reading when I was two years old. I like to learn about the weather like tornadoes, earthquakes floods, and hurricanes. I want to be an Astrogeologists when I grow up. I really love science. I would like to thank my Dad and Mom for being the best parents in the world.

www.ingramcontent.com/pod-product-compliance
Lightning Source LLC
Chambersburg PA
CBHW042252100526
44587CB00002B/108